SCHIRMER PERFORMANCE EDITIONS

CHOPIN
PRELUDES

Edited by Brian Ganz

T0055423

To access companion recorded performances online, visit:
www.halleonard.com/mylibrary

Enter Code
3174-6416-0028-8039

On the cover:
Chopin Playing the Piano in Prince Radziwill's Salon in Berlin (1887)
by Hendryk Siemiradzki
(1843-1902)
© The Bridgeman Art Library/Getty Images

ISBN 978-0-634-08444-7

G. SCHIRMER, *Inc.*

DISTRIBUTED BY

HAL•LEONARD®
CORPORATION
7777 W. BLUEMOUND RD. P.O. BOX 13819 MILWAUKEE, WI 53213

www.musicsalesclassical.com
www.halleonard.com

CONTENTS

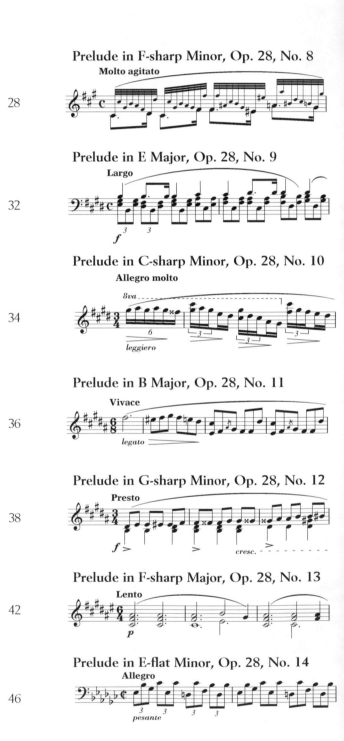

HISTORICAL NOTES

FRÉDÉRIC FRANÇOIS CHOPIN (1810-1849)

Chopin was a pivotal figure in the history of the piano. He wrote music ideally suited to the "new" piano that was evolving during his life. As a result of developments in piano technology, the new instruments were capable of producing a broader palate of colors than their predecessors. They also allowed pianists to execute much faster, more intricate, delicate passage work than earlier instruments. Chopin used these elements of the new instruments, along with the sound-altering capabilities of the instrument's *una corda* pedal, to create music full of subtly interwoven melodies and colorful, modal harmonies. He established the piano as a solo instrument, performing his own fluid, expressive music with a delicate touch and tremendous sensitivity. Virtually all of his compositions were either pieces for solo piano or pieces that featured the piano prominently.

Born near Warsaw, Poland, to a Polish mother and a French father, Chopin was an undeniable prodigy. The boy's precocious playing opened the doors of Warsaw salons, where he quickly became the darling of society, and reveled in the elegance and style of that world. Chopin began writing music as a child as well, publishing his first pieces at age seven. Following his education at the Warsaw Conservatory, he left Poland for Vienna in 1830 to make a name for himself in the cultural capital. But he eventually settled in Paris, where he became a sought-after teacher and, once again, a favorite performer in the salons of the wealthy and aristocratic, where educated, cultured people gathered to hear the latest music, poetry, or literature of the day.

Famous for his fussy, fashionable clothing and handsome face, Chopin led a pampered life. A small, frail man weighing just over 100 pounds, he was quite sensitive about his physical stature because he felt it kept him from making as big a sound on the piano as he, and his critics, would have liked. Accordingly, Chopin enjoyed playing in the small salons, or drawing rooms, of wealthy music lovers. He felt these spaces were suited to his relatively small sound and they did not cause him the nervous tension he felt when playing in large halls. In fact, Chopin's legendary reputation as a performer stems from a total of about 30 public, concert-hall performances over the course of his entire career. Chopin preferred to be known as a composer, a reputation Robert Schumann helped build by writing, in a review of Chopin's *Variations*, Op. 2, "Hats off, gentlemen, a genius!"

Chopin was never able to return to Poland, due to political upheaval and war there, and he always missed his homeland deeply. He incorporated some of the folk music he heard as a youth into lovely, longing pieces of music. Although he never married, Chopin carried on a nearly decade-long affair with the bold novelist George Sand (Aurore Dudevant). She lived a wildly bohemian, outspoken lifestyle, smoking cigars and dressing in men's clothing. But she became a tender, maternal care-giver to the composer, creating the happiest, most productive period of his life. Chopin's frail health, diminished by tuberculosis, deteriorated during their years together, plummeting after their break-up. He died two years later, at age 39, and was buried in Paris. Mozart's *Requiem* was performed at his funeral, which was attended by almost 3,000 people.

—Elaine Schmidt

PERFORMANCE NOTES

Some General Comments

The *Preludes* of Frédéric Chopin are among the most beloved works in all of piano literature, and among the most often studied and performed. In no other works is Chopin's genius for brevity and poetry on more vivid display. In no other works are there such varied levels of difficulty, offering gratification to the near beginner as well as challenge to the seasoned professional. And in no other works does Chopin explore as large or as satisfying a range of emotional states.

But although the *Preludes'* nearly universal affection and widespread familiarity are well deserved, they come with a price. For sometimes a piece we hear frequently becomes harder and harder to hear *truly*. It is as if a kind of cellophane or plastic wrap begins to grow around the music, and listening to it can be like eating food we have forgotten to remove from its packaging. If a piece reaches this stage in our experience, we are likely to say it has grown stale and put it aside for a while, perhaps for good. But what if there were a way to tear off the cellophane and interact with the piece with both the skill born of familiarity and the thrill of first-time discovery?

In this edition of the Chopin *Preludes* I have endeavored to offer the pianist tools for removing the cellophane from these much loved and familiar pieces and discovering their originality anew. Although I have taken a "less is more" approach to the score itself, seeking to preserve a relatively direct contact between composer and performer, I have sought in the performance notes to share insights both about the preludes themselves and about this very process of rediscovery. Such rediscovery involves the stimulation and exercise of what may be new musical "muscles" for some: asking provocative questions, reading "between the lines," and attempting to enter the mind of Chopin as he decides to go here instead of there, this way instead of that. These pursuits involve imaginative and creative skills that we often neglect in the face of the enormous challenges of refined pianism, but I believe we neglect them at great cost to our musical souls.

Thus, the user of this edition may expect to encounter many questions throughout the performance notes, some answered, some left unanswered. The goal of such questions is not just to provide information but also to stimulate creative thinking. There is indeed much to think about, and learning how to *think well* about music is an essential aspect of learning to play it well. Asking skillful questions – reading "between the lines" – getting inside the mind of the composer: these are the overarching motives of this new edition.

The Score and the Recording

I have based this edition on the manuscript Chopin completed in Majorca in January of 1839, and although the manuscript is not entirely free of errors, as we shall see, it is unusually beautiful and instructive. I present the information contained in this manuscript in all its elegant economy. Dynamics, slurs, pedal indications, verbal directions, hairpin *crescendos* and *diminuendos*, even Chopin's sometimes surprising chord and note spellings, all have been meticulously reproduced. I have changed, or added, very little. The very few changes are without exception noted and explained in the performance notes. The occasional additions are solely for the purpose of clarifying Chopin's intentions where the manuscript leaves them incomplete or in doubt, and are usually set in brackets. Where brackets are not feasible, the additions are explained in the notes.

I wish to acknowledge, in addition to the manuscript, the reference sources I've consulted to create this edition: the (Polish) National Edition of Jan Ekier, and the Henle Urtext. I have also learned an enormous amount from the extensive commentary in the Paderewski edition and have benefited from an examination of the edition of Chopin's pupil Carl Mikuli.

Another source that has guided my work on this edition is the knowledge gained from the "field of play," the concert stage. I have performed these works for many years and have also recorded them, and I am eager to pass on what this experience has taught me.

I would like to comment here on the recording included in this edition. For an aspiring artist, listening to any recording represents something of a danger and an opportunity. The opportunity is that a sound picture, no less than a visual one, is worth the proverbial thousand words. The danger is that the listener might take the recording too literally and attempt to copy exactly what I have done, undermining my primary aim of guiding the pianist to his or her own personal and creative relationship with the *Preludes*. Listeners should bear in mind that the recording offers one possible realization among many, a musical snapshot if you will, taken in January of 2001. A performer's career encompasses an entire "album" of such snapshots, and no two of these will be identical, for performers are themselves students who continue to learn and discover throughout their lives, always adding new layers of understanding. My work on this edition has added many such layers.

Fingering

When I considered the issue of fingerings for this edition, I settled on the motto: "First show them how I might solve the problem, then let them solve it for themselves." As a teacher, I am acutely aware of the danger of offering too much assistance when a student is eager to solve his or her own problems. Hence, I offer most fingering suggestions toward the beginning of a prelude and pass the baton to the user of this edition toward the end. Of course, there is always more than one way to finger a passage well. What I offer are suggestions only, and frequently a second possibility is noted in parentheses.

Pianists may note my fondness for finger substitutions. There are several accounts of Chopin's having instructed his own students to strive for a sensuous relationship between the fingers and the keys. For example, as Jean-Jacques Eigeldinger reports in *Chopin: Pianist and Teacher* (1986), Chopin advised one student to "caress the key, never bash it." Finger substitutions are one way of cultivating this caress, often involving a delicious slide along the key.

Pedaling

Pedaling was without doubt the most problematic issue throughout the preparation of this edition. The problems derived from the inherent inexactness of the symbols Chopin used, a slightly flowery "ped." for depression (𝓟𝓮𝓭.) and a large oval with a cross through it for release (⊕), to say nothing of his occasional mild sloppiness. For example, sometimes the music for each hand is placed at slightly different points along a horizontal axis, and one is left wondering whether a pedal mark is meant to occur at the appropriate point in the left or right hand. Chopin famously disliked the tedium of writing down his ideas. By the time he was ready to add pedal markings he may well have been too tired of the whole process to care much about precision.

Rather than leave the markings in this state of imprecision, I have chosen to use a clear, modern pedal indication, a horizontal line with precise depress and release points. ⌞——∧———∧——⌟ This also makes continuous *legato* pedaling easy to represent.

When interpreting Chopin's pedal markings, the pianist must keep in mind a historical factor concerning the type of piano Chopin used in comparison to today's instruments. Although advances in piano construction considerably increased the expressive potential of pianos in Chopin's time, modern cast-iron frames were not integral to their structure until the mid-19th century. With the heavier metal frame came a great deal more tension on the strings, much more power in the projection of tone, and greater blur in longer pedaling. Chopin, writing for instruments with weaker frames, often wrote longer pedal markings than would normally be employed on today's instruments.

In spite of these historical factors, I have chosen to translate Chopin's pedal markings as faithfully and accurately as possible into our precise indications. The pianist deserves, after all, to be aware of Chopin's original intentions. Where these markings would seem less appropriate for modern instruments, or where Chopin's indications seem incomplete, I offer alternative suggestions under the heading "Pedaling Possibilities" in the individual performance notes.

Ornamentation

I suggest a non-dogmatic approach regarding the interpretation of ornaments in Chopin's *Preludes*. The very nature of ornamentation places it in the realm of the spontaneous, the improvised, where Chopin of course reigned supreme. It is unlikely that he ever played ornaments exactly the same way twice. That said, I have reproduced Chopin's ornamentation exactly as he wrote it in the manuscript, even when he writes similar ornaments in different ways within the same prelude. For example, in the two excerpts below, note the different rhythmic values for each ornament, and the missing slur in the second excerpt.

Prelude No. 24: m. 7, r.h.

Prelude No. 24: m. 25, r.h.

I also follow precisely Chopin's inclusion or exclusion of cross-strokes on all grace notes. However, one may fairly ask what significance these cross-strokes have in Chopin's music, since he was far from consistent in their use. The answer is likely, "only a little." Broadly speaking, there are four possibilities for the execution of grace notes, whether they have cross-strokes or not. They may be played quickly before the beat, quickly on the beat, slowly (or at least more expressively) before the beat, and slowly (or more expressively) on the beat. The presence or absence of a cross-stroke may provide a clue to the intended execution of a grace note. It does seem to me that Chopin is somewhat more likely to use cross-strokes in faster tempos, where the ornaments are likely to be played quickly and before the beat. Where he does not use cross-strokes, the grace notes seem somewhat more likely intended as *appoggiaturas*, to be played expressively, and on the beat. However, there are exceptions; hence the non-dogmatic approach.

Several ornaments in the *Preludes* warrant further discussion. Shorter ones have been realized in the score itself. The remaining are addressed here.

In Prelude No. 8, m. 34, I recommend that the ornament be performed in this manner:

Prelude No. 8: mm. 33-34

Another possible realization:

Prelude No. 8: mm. 33-34

Prelude No. 9 merits special consideration due to variant rhythmic notations for its signature rhythmic figure.

Example A (first edition):

The first edition and many subsequent publications notate this rhythmic figure as shown above, with the sixteenth note set apart from the lower-voice triplet throughout. This notation implies that the sixteenth note is to be played after the final eighth of the triplet, and indeed, it is most often performed that way. However, in Chopin's manuscript this figure is written as in Example B below, allowing for a different interpretation.

Example B (manuscript):

Note that in this version, the sixteenth note is to be played simultaneously with the final eighth of the triplet. If the performer adopts this version of the prelude, I recommend that the upper voice in beat 1, m. 8 be played as a duplet against the lower-voice triplet:

Prelude No. 9: m. 8, beats 1-2

For m. 4, the usual execution, following the first-edition version, is as follows, with the grace notes before the trill played either on the beat or before the beat:

Prelude No. 9: m. 4, beat 4

However, if the manuscript variant is applied, the ornament may be played thus:

Prelude No. 9: m. 4, beat 4

If the first-edition notation is followed, the ornamental notes that follow the trill should be played with the sixteenth note.

Prelude No. 9: m. 3, beats 3-4; m. 4, beat 1

But if the manuscript's rhythmic interpretation is adopted:

Prelude No. 9: m. 3, beats 3-4; m. 4, beat 1

The final LH notes of m. 3 may also be played after the final RH chord.

In Prelude No. 13, m. 7, the E♯ should follow the G♯, thus:

Prelude No. 13: m. 7

Here, the placement of the ornamental roll with respect to the LH accompaniment is left to the discretion of the performer. For example, the roll may begin on the beat (the RH F♯ coincides with the LH downbeat) or before the beat (the RH D♯ coincides with the LH downbeat). Another possibility, which I favor, is to place the grace note E♯ with the LH downbeat, thus:

Prelude No. 13: m. 7

In mm. 33-36 of the same prelude, I recommend that the RH chords be played on the beat, with the upper voice entering just afterwards. For example:

Prelude No. 13: m. 33

In Prelude No. 23, m. 2, the LH grace notes may be aligned with the final sixteenth note of the beat:

Prelude No. 23: m. 2

Alternatively, the grace notes before the trill may be played on the beat. Likewise, the grace notes before the trill in m. 7 of Prelude No. 10 may also be played on or before the beat.

In sum, many factors should be considered when deciding how to execute a Chopin ornament: the mood of the prelude, the level of dissonance in the ornament, the tempo, the presence or absence of cross-strokes, historical performance practice, etc. The student or performer should experiment with various possibilities and then have a good reason for his or her choice. I will make frequent recommendations in the individual performance notes.

Phrase Structure

In the individual notes for each prelude, I suggest a possible diagram of the phrase structure for consideration. It is particularly interesting to note where Chopin departs from the usual 4- or 8- bar phrase. When a longer phrase encompasses several smaller segments, I place a possible segmentation in parentheses. Particularly interesting phrase or segment lengths are noted with an exclamation point. The structure is outlined quite broadly, however, in groups of whole measures. The student is encouraged to parse the phrase structure in greater detail.

The Individual Preludes: A Preview of the Online Notes

We have elected to put the performance notes for the individual preludes online rather than in the printed text. This decision has several advantages for the student. The unrestricted space of the online format permits us to furnish detailed information gleaned from a close examination of the manuscript, much of which would be unwieldy in printed form. Also, with online notes we are free to include the kinds of analytical observations and questions that, ideally, will spark the student's own interpretive insights. Thus, this edition will serve as an interactive educational tool in a way impractical for a normal printed edition. (Go to **www.halleonard. com/item_detail.jsp?itemid=296523** and click on the *Closer Look* icon.)

To introduce the user of this edition to the structure and various features of the online notes, I offer the following preview of the notes for Preludes 4, 7, and 8, followed by corresponding passages from the Appendix for Prelude No. 4. Each detailed exploration of the individual preludes follows this format:

- a general discussion of the prelude and its most interesting features
- specific comments elucidating various aspects of the score
- pedaling possibilities
- suggested phrase structure
- questions for the student's further exploration (Responses to these questions are furnished in the Appendix.)

PRELUDE NO. 4

Chopin demonstrates his unique contrapuntal gift in this prelude. This is unquestionably a prelude of great melodic beauty, and yet if we play the right hand by itself the line feels static, almost dull. Chopin gives the line life by creating great interest in the LH chords, and in so doing invests the accompaniment with a counter-melodic strength. With each successive chord change, one (or occasionally two) of the chordal notes descends a whole, or more commonly, a half step. The descent occurs in no particular pattern and in no discernible order, resulting in many chords that do not function according to traditional harmonic practice, and herein lies their fascination. For example, in a work in E minor, we would expect the left-hand D7 chord in m. 7 to resolve to the relative-major key of G if it were functioning normally. In this prelude's tonal world, this chord functions entirely differently, but with no less convincing a musical logic. The static right-hand melodic line "borrows," as it were, the compelling allure of the throbbing left-hand chords. The melodic line comes into its own more vivid beauty around m. 8, precisely when the chords below return to traditional tonal function, no longer needed for their nonfunctional fascination. This is an entirely different counterpoint from that of Chopin's first love, Bach, the contrapuntal master *nonpareil*, and yet it is clearly informed and inspired by it.

The word *largo* means "broad" in Italian. The three preludes marked *largo* (the E major, C minor, and this one) suggest that for Chopin (at least in the *Preludes*) *largo* indicates a striding tempo with a broad "gait." (In general, Chopin's *lento* would seem to indicate a somewhat slower tempo. See the note for Prelude No. 6.) Keep in mind that this prelude is to be felt broadly in two, not in four, as it is marked ¢ or "cut time."

Compare the accompaniment of this prelude to that of the *Mazurka in A minor, Op. 17, No. 4*, composed a few years before the *Preludes*. That mazurka may have been a kind of creative seed for this prelude.

Mazurka, Op. 17, No. 4: mm. 8-11, l.h.

Prelude No. 4: mm. 1-4, l.h.

Identifying similar passages or principles in different works is one of the keys to entering the mental processes of the composer. (See also the note for Prelude No. 14.)

MM. 8, 12: No better illustrations exist for my adage, "A Chopin accent is always more than an accent," than the two accents in these measures. Can you find something novel about these accented notes, something which may have inspired Chopin to accent them, beyond the call, simply, for greater volume? This novelty is the key to interpreting the accent convincingly. Consider m. 12: Notice that the accented C is the first note since the chords were introduced in m. 1 to be played *without accompaniment*. Awareness of this might encourage the performer to play this lonely note more soulfully and more searchingly, perhaps even more painfully, than the surrounding notes, and not merely more loudly. Can you see what is novel about the G♯ of m. 8? (See the Appendix for a possible answer.)

Alternatively, it is possible to interpret the accents in these measures as *diminuendo* "hairpins," rather than accents. Often the two are indistinguishable in Chopin's manuscripts, and one must use context and instinct to determine his intent. Different interpretations are valid. For example, both the Henle edition and that of Chopin's pupil Carl Mikuli interpret the mark in m. 8 as a *diminuendo*, and both editions consider the mark in m. 12 an accent. Ekier gives the marks in *both* measures as accents, as does Paderewski, but in Ekier's edition they are slightly larger than normal size.

M. 12: What makes this measure so poignantly beautiful? I believe it has something to do with the close juxtaposition of the raised 7th degree of the scale and the lowered 7th, in this case the D♯ and the D♮. This is a favorite expressive device of Chopin's.

Prelude No. 4: m. 12, r.h.

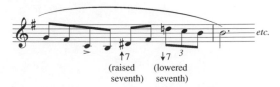

Can you find other instances of this juxtaposition in the *Preludes*? An instance quite similar to this one occurs in Prelude No. 16, m. 17, just before the return to the opening material. Look for a very different, but no less exquisite occurrence, in Prelude No. 6, mm. 21-22.

M. 14: Consider that there are often slight differences between otherwise similar phrases. For example, compare m. 14 to m. 2 and note the expressive difference. Sometimes, listening deeply and responding *consciously* to the difference between varied points in similar phrases is all that is necessary to project that difference beautifully and convincingly. To focus on these subtle differences, juxtapose them, playing them immediately after one another. For example, here play m. 2, and then immediately play m. 14. As you play, be conscious of the difference between the two phrases, and your listener will be as well.

M. 24: This is the first instance of the dynamic *pianissimo* in the *Preludes*. Be sure to highlight it.

Pedaling Possibilities
It seems odd that Chopin indicates only two instances of pedal in this prelude. The two instances share something in common: They involve the only departures from repeated chords in the accompaniment. In both cases, the LH descends for a deeper bass-anchor that Chopin wants sustained. However, I believe this prelude offers evidence that Chopin sometimes considers use of the pedal to be so obvious that its explicit indication is unnecessary. Note the slurs over the LH chords, suggesting a *legato* articulation. This *legato* would be impossible with repeated chords if no pedal were used at all. Experiment with light *legato* pedal, changing it fractionally on every 8th note, or changing less frequently (for a richer sound) to taste. The final chords can use a deeper pedal for *legato* and resonance.

Possible Phrase Structure
MM. 1-12 (1-4, 5-8, 9-12); 13-25 (13-16, 17-20, 21-25)

For Further Exploration
What is extraordinary about the first chord in this prelude?

Does the 5-bar phrase at the end of this prelude (see mm. 21-25) affect you in the same way as the 5-bar phrase from Prelude No. 3 (see mm. 7-11)? Why, or why not?

Have you ever spelled a word wrong on a test? Is there a chord in this prelude which Chopin may have "misspelled"? What does it mean to misspell a chord?

PRELUDE NO. 7
This is a miniature mazurka! One of the characteristic mazurka rhythms is a dotted-eighth/sixteenth note on the first beat of a 3/4 measure, and we see that rhythm consistently here.

Prelude No. 7: mm. 1-2, r.h.

Mazurka, Op. 17, No. 4: mm. 5-6, r.h.

The second example above is excerpted from the opening measures of the *Mazurka in A Minor, Op. 17, No. 4*, also cited in the notes for Prelude No. 4. Note the rhythmic similarity of the two examples.

For Chopin, the marking *Andantino* suggested a tempo slightly faster than *Andante*. However, it is worth noting that in the manuscript Chopin appears to have written *Andante* originally. He then crossed it out and wrote *Andantino* instead. It may be valid, therefore, to perform this prelude on the slower side of *Andantino*, in recognition of Chopin's original impulse.

Note that the two long phrases in this prelude comprise eight phrase segments of identical rhythm. Could this repetitive rhythm have inspired Chopin, either consciously or unconsciously, to experiment in the following prelude (No. 8) with absolutely no rhythmic differentiation between beats, over 32 measures?

Given that this is one of the shortest works that Chopin ever composed, it is worth considering here the nature of Chopin's genius for brevity. One essential characteristic of this genius is the knowledge of *what to leave out*. For an imagination as fertile as Chopin's, this is no small matter. There is an amusing illustration of this phenomenon in the literary world. The French mathematician and philosopher Blaise Pascal once wrote an exceptionally long letter to a friend, at the end of which he apologized because *he didn't have time to write a shorter one*!

Pedaling Possibilities
The construction of the modern piano is relevant to the performance of this prelude. On a modern instrument, the pedaling as Chopin gives it usually sounds too blurred. I recommend a slight clearance of the pedal just after the dotted rhythm, lifting up the pedal about one-half of the way before re-depressing it.

Prelude No. 7: mm. 1-4

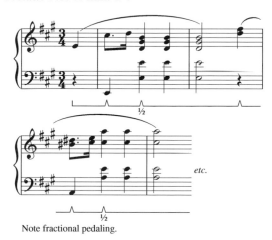

Note fractional pedaling.

Also, as this excerpt shows, I recommend pedaling from the pickup to the downbeat (where Chopin indicates no pedal), both for consistency of sound and also for a better *legato* when the pickup and the downbeat are the same notes. Change the pedal, of course, on the downbeat.

Possible Phrase Structure
MM. 1-8 (1-4, 5-8); 9-16 (9-12, 13-16)

For Further Exploration
This prelude offers an opportunity to develop an important aspect of musical insight: the capacity to see something new in comparable phrases. The performer who remains conscious of these nuances throughout the piece will communicate them to the listener, who will be aware of them as elements of an unfolding story. In each of the eight phrase segments, determine what is happening for the first time. (See also the note for Prelude No. 2.)

PRELUDE NO. 8

Though several of the preludes possess very little rhythmic variation, this one is impressive (and rare among Chopin's works) for the sheer quantity of notes uninterrupted by even the slightest change in rhythm in either hand: 32 measures comprising 128 beats, or 1,536 notes, without any rhythmic variation among them! Why is this significant? In addition to highlighting the extraordinary degree of harmonic and melodic richness and invention of this prelude, it also makes the curious rhythmic variety throughout the subsequent prelude (No. 9) all the more interesting and satisfying. I offer this juxtaposition as evidence of the likelihood that Chopin had sequential performance of the *Preludes* in mind when he conceived them.

Chopin was a master chromaticist. His capacity to wend his way through a forest of richly varied keys without appearing to meander or lose direction was without parallel. In this prelude, he seems almost to be showing off this gift. There are nineteen key changes, either firm or fleeting, in the first sixteen bars!

As in the first prelude, the performer has the option of occasionally highlighting the upper voice (i.e., the second and eighth of the 32nd notes in each beat).

Prelude No. 8: m. 9, r.h.

The arrows point to a voice which may be highlighted occasionally to taste.

Chopin makes explicit a similar expressive shift in voicing in the *Fantaisie-Impromptu, Op. 66.* However, Chopin's notation of this prelude makes clear that the lower of the two voices is the primary melody. He underscores this intent by writing a note in French to his publisher, directly on the manuscript, stating that it is mandatory to distinguish in print between the large and small notes.

In his fine work *The Literature of the Piano* (1948), Ernest Hutcheson points out the need for a highly expressive right thumb in performing this prelude.

MM. 1-2: I believe Chopin intends the LH *diminuendos* in these measures to carry through to measure 33.

MM. 6, 20: Note the new interval that concludes the second beat of each of these measures. Some editions dismiss the change as a slip on Chopin's part and adjust the final A of these beats to F♯. (I learned this prelude with such an edition; consequently, you will not hear the correct interval in my recording.) The manuscript makes clear, however, that the change is no slip. Contrary to his usual practice of indicating the repetition of previous material with symbols directing the publisher to repeat the appropriate measures, Chopin notates the music of mm. 5 and 6 anew in mm. 19 and 20. He repeats, quite clearly, the unexpected tenth that concludes the 2nd beat of mm. 6 and 20.

M. 9: Some editions give the second LH note of the third beat as G♮, which would serve as the dominant of C minor over the pedal point F. (I learned it this way myself; you will hear G♮ in the recording.) The manuscript, however, is clear: Only in the *next* beat does Chopin make it a G♮, as part of the C minor chord. Chopin's intentions here would have been clearer had he spelled the G♯ as A♭ (as he does in the RH), which resolves logically in the next beat to the G♮ (as does the RH A♭).

MM. 25-26: The hairpin-like symbols in these two measures are clearly distinguished from those in mm. 1-2. Those in mm. 1-2 are without question *diminuendos*; the symbols in mm. 25-26 are without question accents. For the first time in this prelude, a finger besides the right thumb sees some melodic action. Be sure to highlight the change.

M. 33: The second chord of this measure is a Neapolitan chord in its customary first inversion. Note how it proceeds directly to the dominant. Can you find an earlier occurrence of the Neapolitan chord in this prelude? Does that one move directly to the dominant?

Pedaling Possibilities

I have interpreted Chopin's pedal markings here as *legato* pedaling, although in the manuscript there is often more than the usual amount of space between the release symbol and the subsequent "ped." indication. My interpretation presumes a slight imprecision on Chopin's part and allows the thumb's melodic line to be played *legato.* If the performer were to take Chopin's marking's quite literally, the pedal would sometimes be released slightly earlier than would be normal in *legato* pedaling, resulting in a "bump" in the *legato.*

Occasionally, Chopin clearly indicates pedaling that lasts longer than a single beat (e.g., in mm. 22, 25 and subsequent measures.) I have reproduced his pedaling faithfully here as elsewhere, though when the pedaling is longer than a single beat I recommend fractional pedal changes to reduce the resulting blur.

Possible phrase structure
MM. 1-4; 5-8; 9-14!; 15-18 (15-16, 17-18); 19-22; 23-26; 27-30 (27-28, 29-30); 31-34 (31-32, 33-34)

For Further Exploration
In the Appendix, I offer my analysis of the keys Chopin settles in or briefly touches throughout this prelude. Analyze the prelude yourself before checking your analysis against mine. Some keys are touched so briefly as to seem mere suggestions; nevertheless, they contribute to the wide spectrum of colors in this prelude.

Determine what very common musical element is missing from this prelude.

Appendix

Here you will find my responses to the questions posed in "For Further Consideration" for Prelude No. 4.

It is important to have a score open to the prelude referenced here, and in the complete online version, so that the concepts and discoveries discussed are readily apparent.

PRELUDE NO. 4
What is extraordinary about the first chord in this prelude?
The first chord of the prelude is in first inversion. Note the rarity of this position for a strong opening statement of the tonic chord. Here we see Chopin on the cutting edge of the transition from Classical to Romantic harmonic practice.

Does the 5-bar phrase at the end of this prelude (see mm. 21-25) affect you in the same way as the 5-bar phrase from Prelude No. 3 (see mm. 7-11)? Why, or why not?
I believe the final phrase of this prelude is not quite a true 5-bar phrase, but rather a 4-bar phrase that resolves, or "reaches," across the bar line. This is not unusual for Chopin, especially in phrases that complete a section or a work. For similar 5-bar phrases consult the "Possible Phrase Structure" for Preludes Nos. 5, 14 and 18, and the *Prelude in C-sharp Minor, Op. 45.* Remember to look toward the end of these preludes.

What is novel, or significant, about the G♯ in m.8?
The accent on the G♯ in m. 8 may serve to highlight the note's significance in ushering in the return of traditional tonality. See how the chords behave briefly as if we have arrived at the key of A minor. Remember that when we are aware of the *significance* of an accented note, the accent will be more than a mere accent.

Have you ever spelled a word wrong on a test? Is there a chord in this prelude which Chopin may have "misspelled"? What does it mean to misspell a chord?
There is a kind of musical "grammar" concerning the *function* of notes or chords; music students must practice understanding this grammar just as they must practice their scales. Is there a C7 chord toward the end of this prelude, as Chopin has spelled it? How would a C7 chord normally resolve? To F major! Does it resolve that way here? No. Another chord containing the same notes as a dominant seventh chord is spelled differently: it is called an augmented 6th chord. In this case the chord should be spelled as an augmented 6th instead of a dominant seventh: the B♭ should be A♯!

The chord as Chopin has spelled it; an inversion of C7:

The chord as Chopin "should" have spelled it; a rearranged augmented 6th:

Here is the chord reconfigured to show the augmented 6th:

It's refreshing, isn't it, that a genius like Chopin may have slipped and forgotten momentarily how a chord's function should determine its spelling! To be fair to Chopin, we should also consider the possibility that he chose to spell the chord with a B♭ because it is easier to read that way. (I have spelled all notes throughout this edition as Chopin did in his manuscript.)

—Brian Ganz

(For responses to the questions posed for Preludes 7 and 8 and all other preludes, consult the online Performance Notes by downloading the PDF at **halleonard.com/mylibrary** using the access code on page 1.)

A son ami Camille Pleyel

Prelude in C Major

Frédéric Chopin
Op. 28, No. 1

Prelude in A Minor

Frédéric Chopin
Op. 28, No. 2

Prelude in G Major

Frédéric Chopin
Op. 28, No. 3

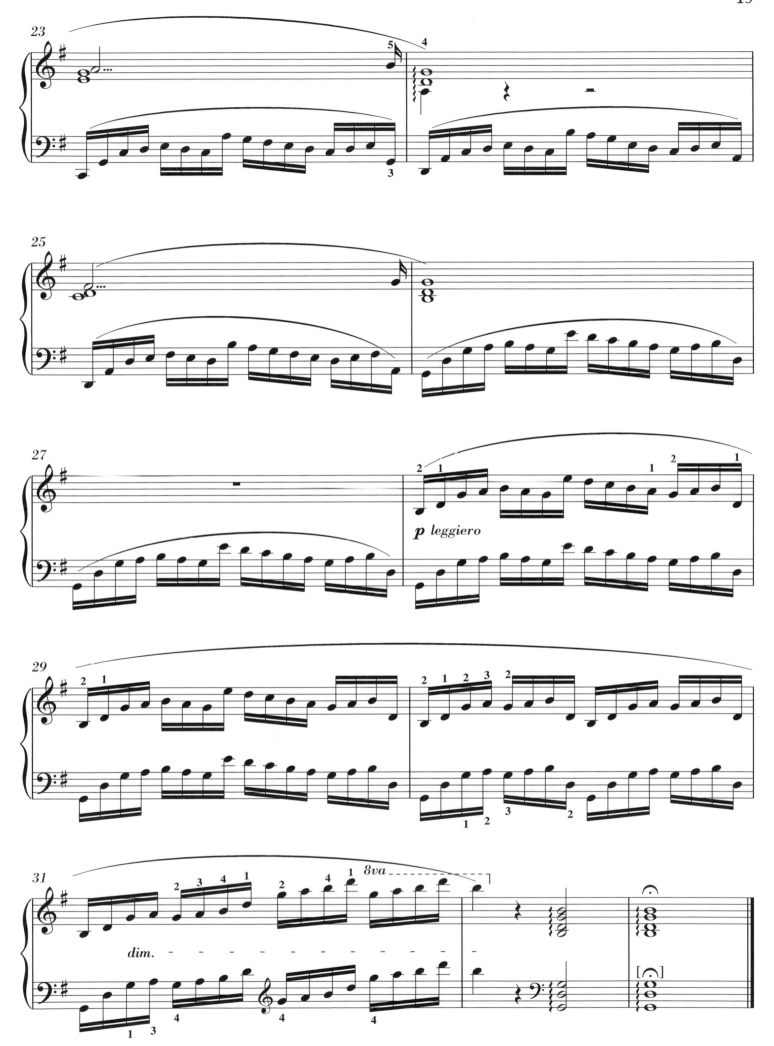

Prelude in E Minor

Frédéric Chopin
Op. 28, No. 4

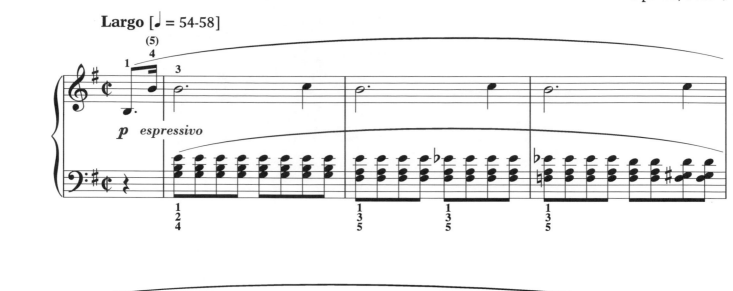

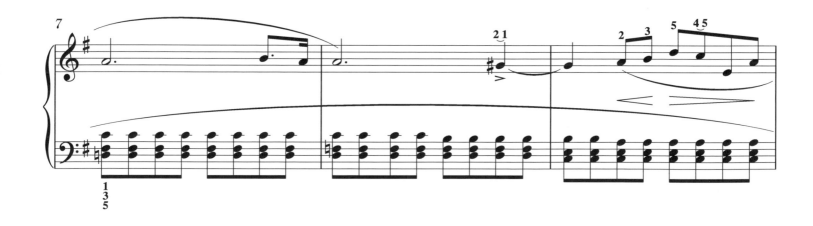

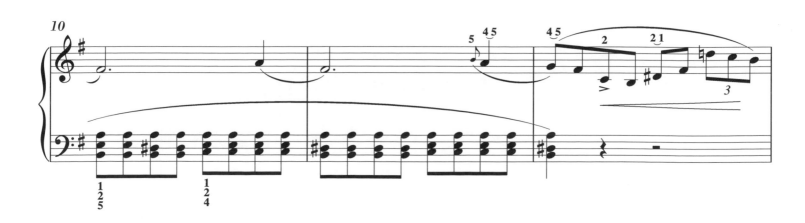

Prelude in D Major

Frédéric Chopin
Op. 28, No. 5

Prelude in B Minor

Frédéric Chopin
Op. 28, No. 6

Prelude in A Major

Frédéric Chopin
Op. 28, No. 7

Prelude in F-sharp Minor

Frédéric Chopin
Op. 28, No. 8

Molto agitato [♩ = 84-88]

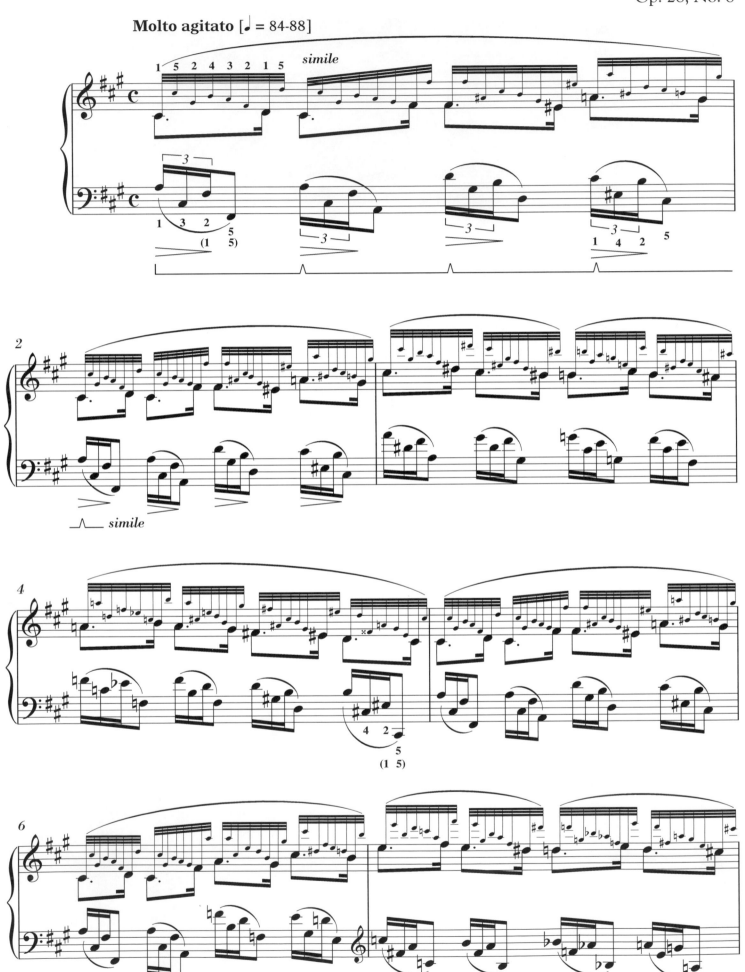

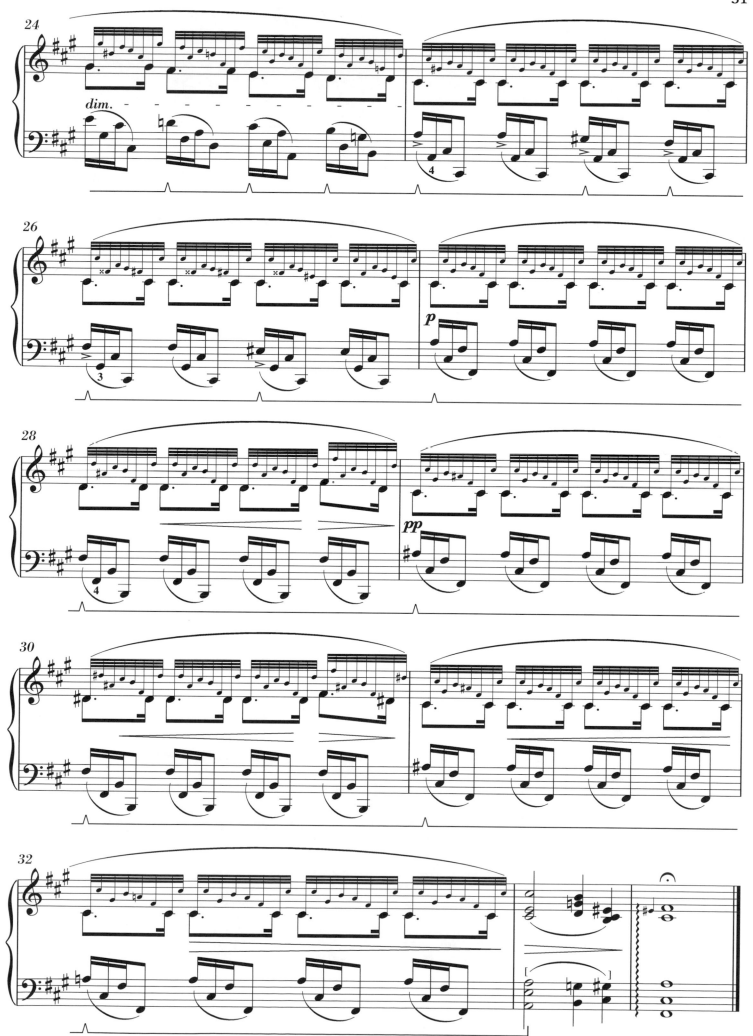

Prelude in E Major

Frédéric Chopin
Op. 28, No. 9

* *We have followed the first-edition notation for this prelude by offsetting the 16th note in this rhythmic figure throughout. However, Chopin's manuscript presents the figure thus:*

If the manuscript version is adopted in performance, all 16ths should be played simultaneously with the final eighth of the lower-voice triplet.

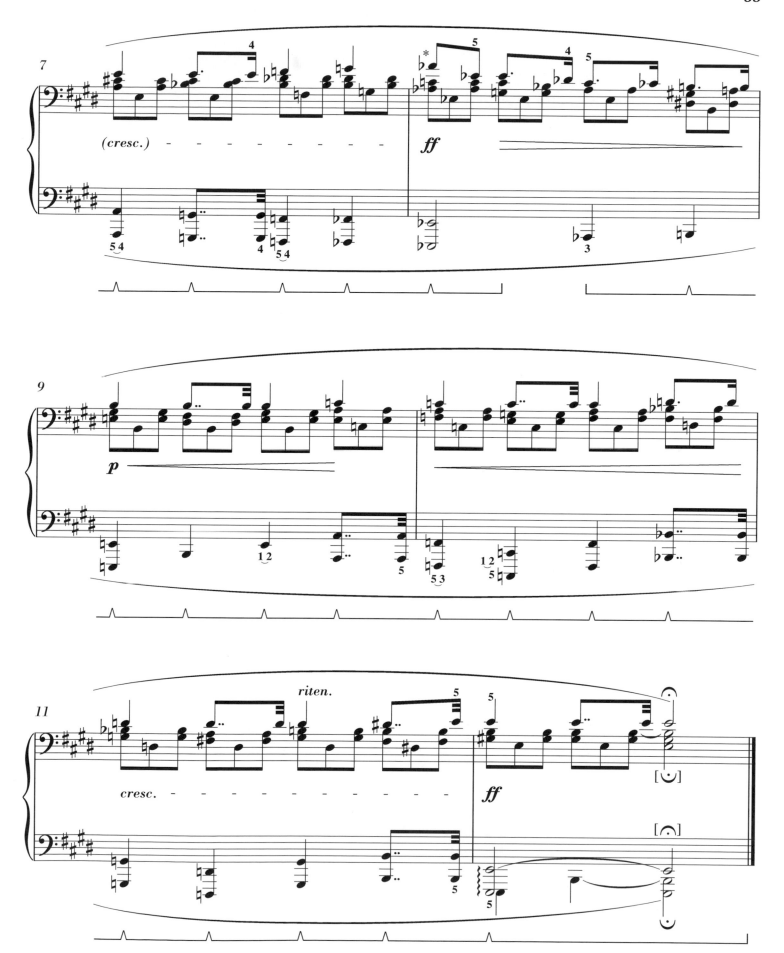

* If the manuscript version is adopted, beat 1, m. 8 should be played thus:

See performance notes p. 7, and also the online notes, for further discussion of this issue.

Prelude in C-sharp Minor

Frédéric Chopin
Op. 28, No. 10

Allegro molto [♩ = 126-144]

Prelude in B Major

Frédéric Chopin
Op. 28, No. 11

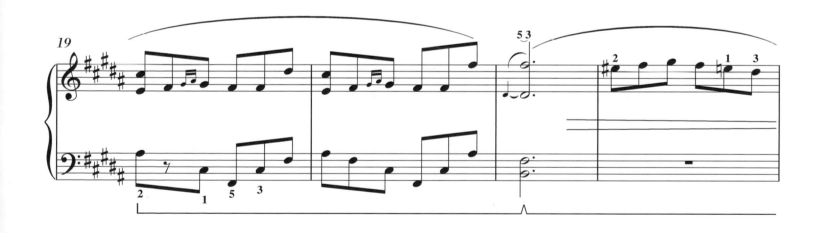

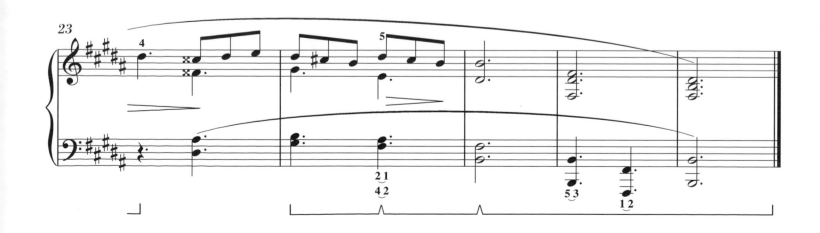

Prelude in G-sharp Minor

Frédéric Chopin
Op. 28, No. 12

Prelude in F-sharp Major

Frédéric Chopin
Op. 28, No. 13

The downstemmed chord is not arpeggiated. The vertical slur indicates the point at which the chord should be broken.

Prelude in E-flat Minor

Frédéric Chopin
Op. 28, No. 14

Prelude in D-flat Major

Frédéric Chopin
Op. 28, No. 15

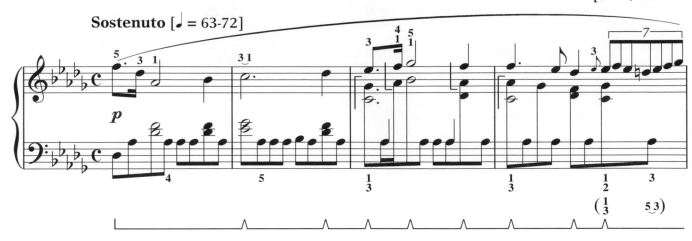

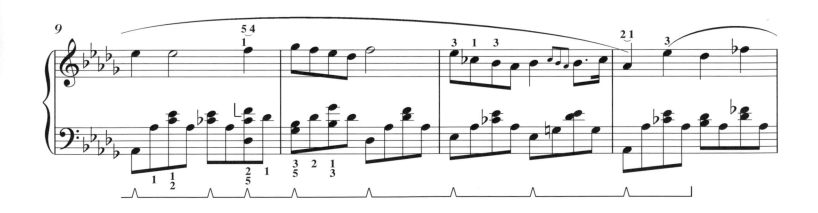

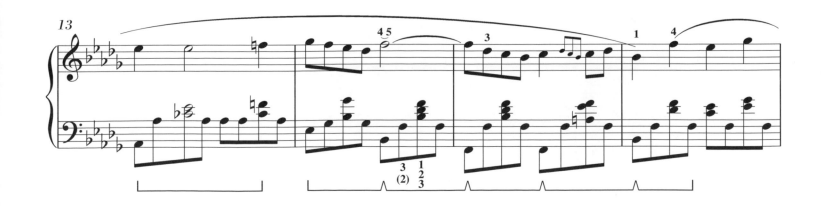

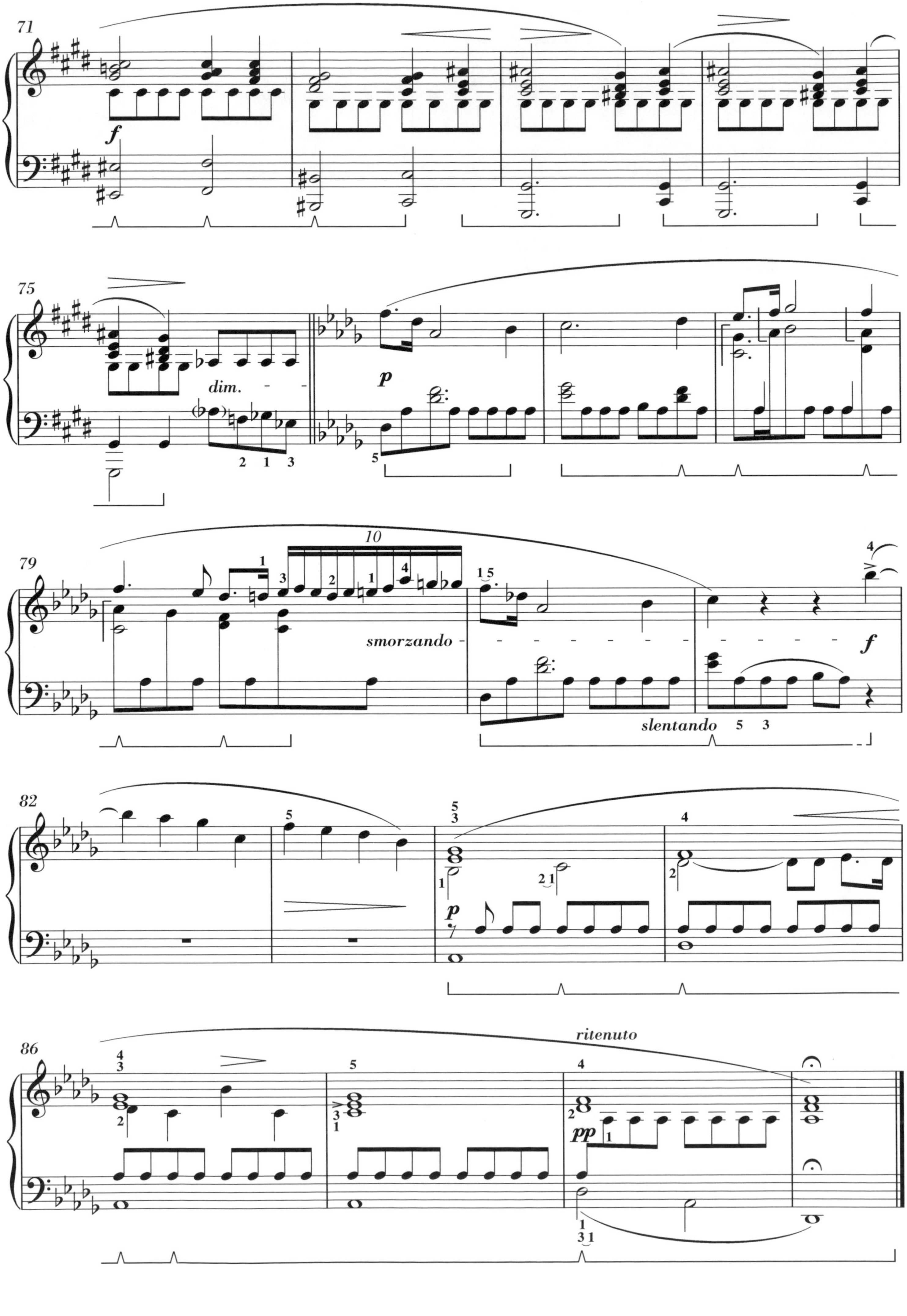
71
75
dim.
79
10
smorzando
slentando
82
86
ritenuto

Prelude in B-flat Minor

Frédéric Chopin
Op. 28, No. 16

Presto con fuoco [♩ = 160-176]

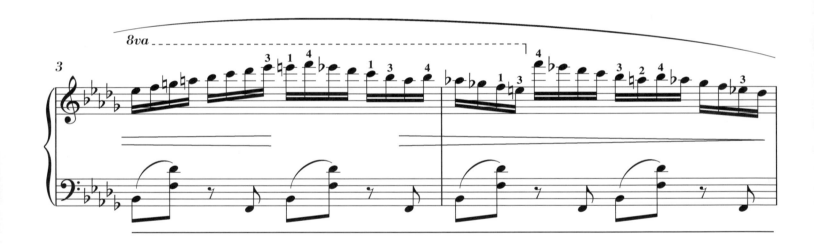

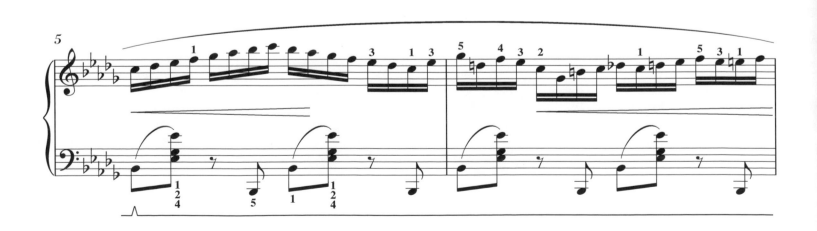

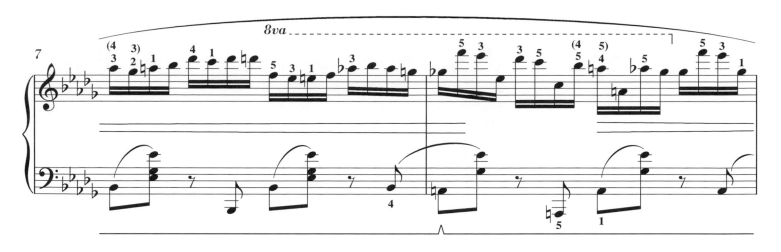

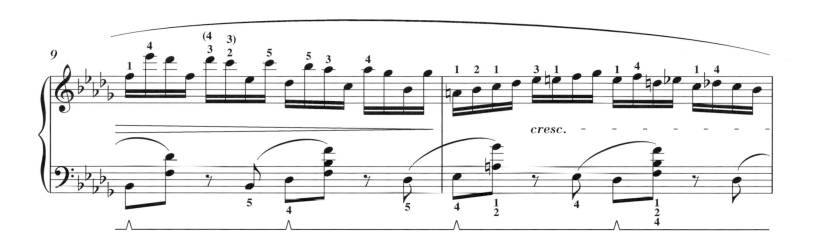

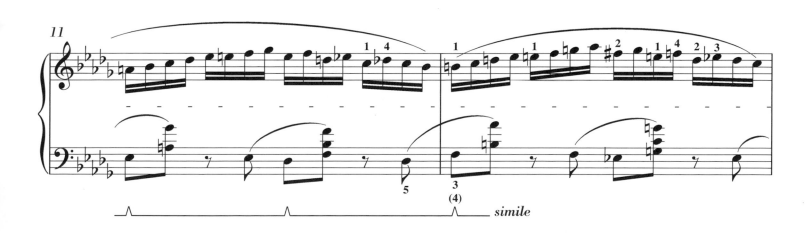

Prelude in A-flat Major

Frédéric Chopin
Op. 28, No. 17

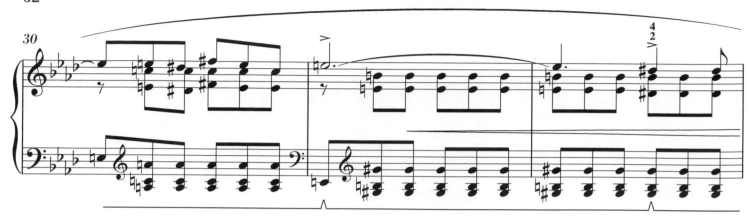

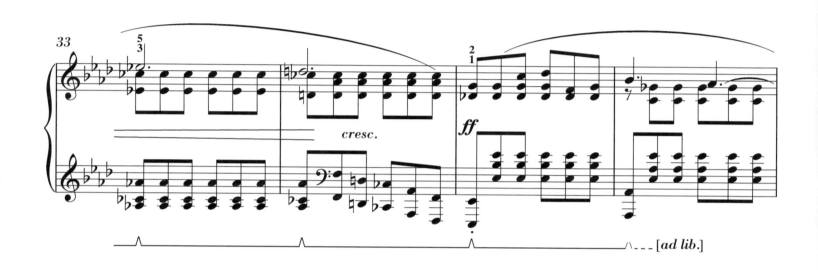

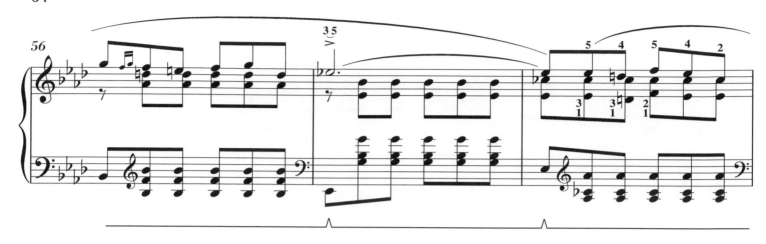

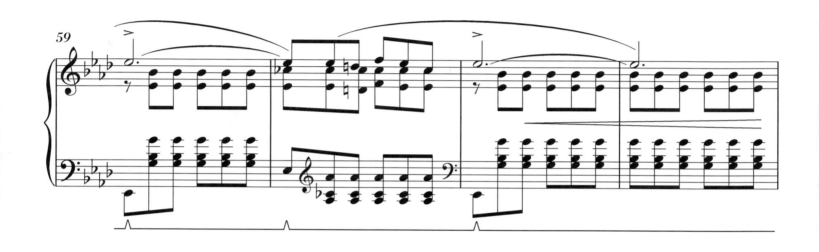

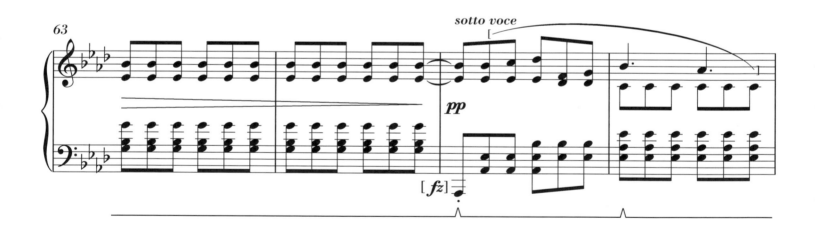

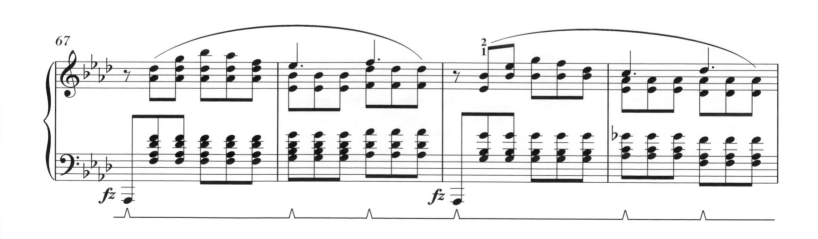

Prelude in F Minor

Frédéric Chopin
Op. 28, No. 18

Allegro molto [♩ = 132-144]

Prelude in E-flat Major

Frédéric Chopin
Op. 28, No. 19

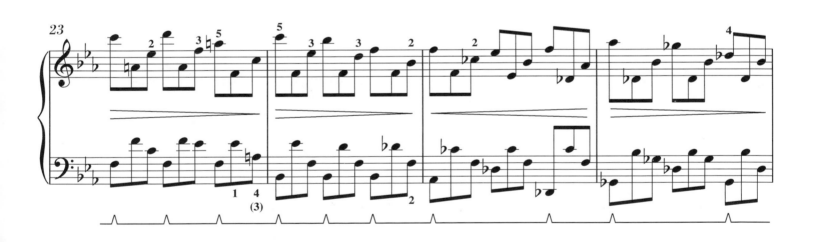

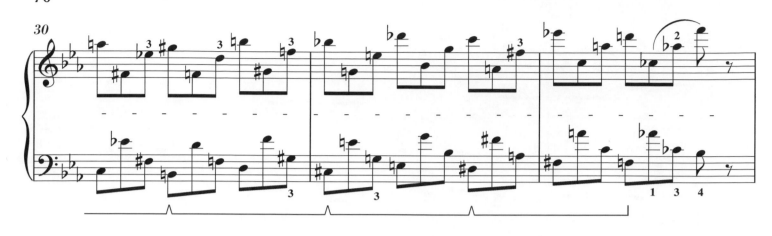

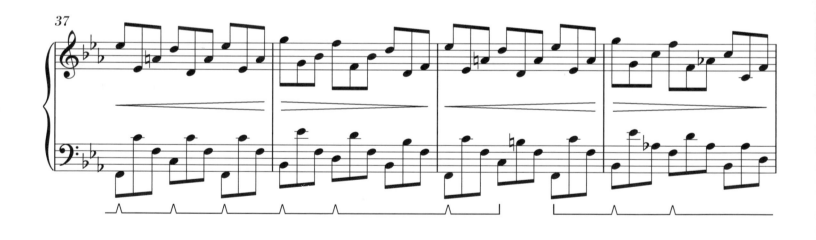

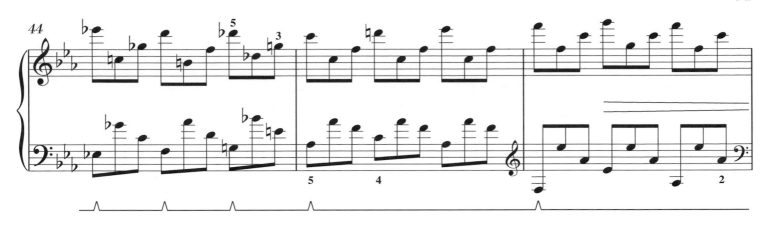

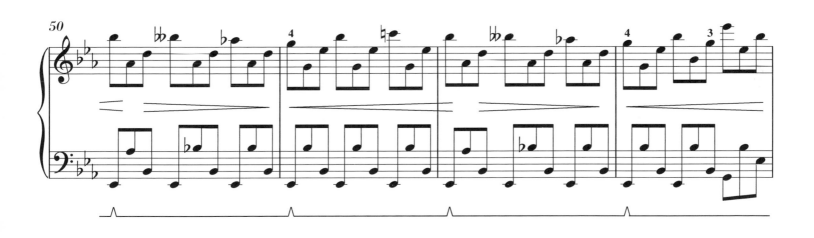

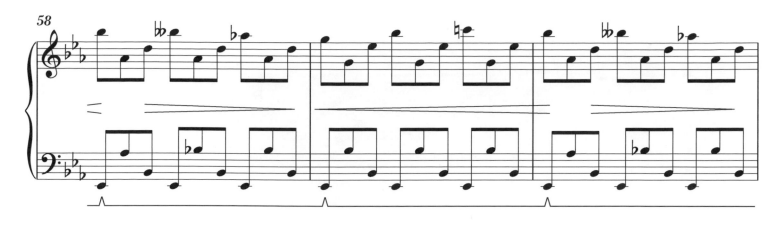

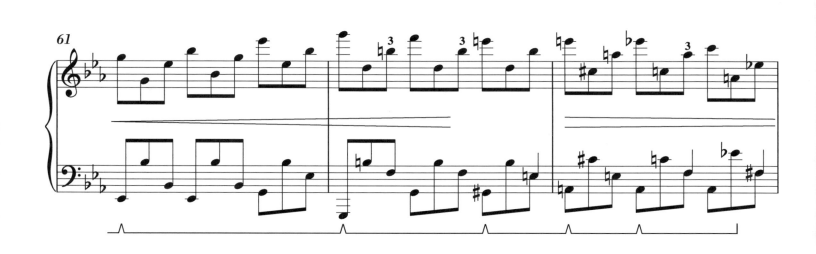

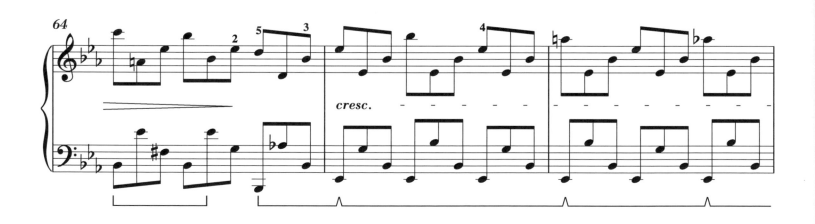

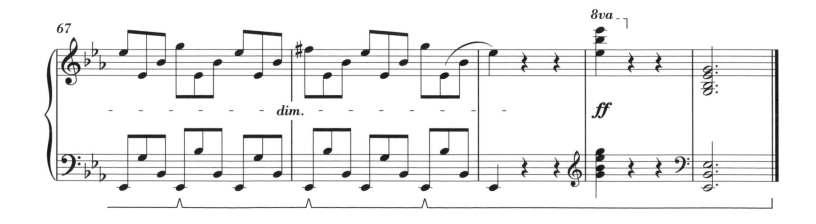

Prelude in C Minor

Frédéric Chopin
Op. 28, No. 20

Largo [♩ = 28-48]

Prelude in B-flat Major

Frédéric Chopin
Op. 28, No. 21

Prelude in G Minor

Frédéric Chopin
Op. 28, No. 22

Molto agitato [♩. = 132-144]

Prelude in F Major

Frédéric Chopin
Op. 28, No. 23

Prelude in D Minor

Frédéric Chopin
Op. 28, No. 24

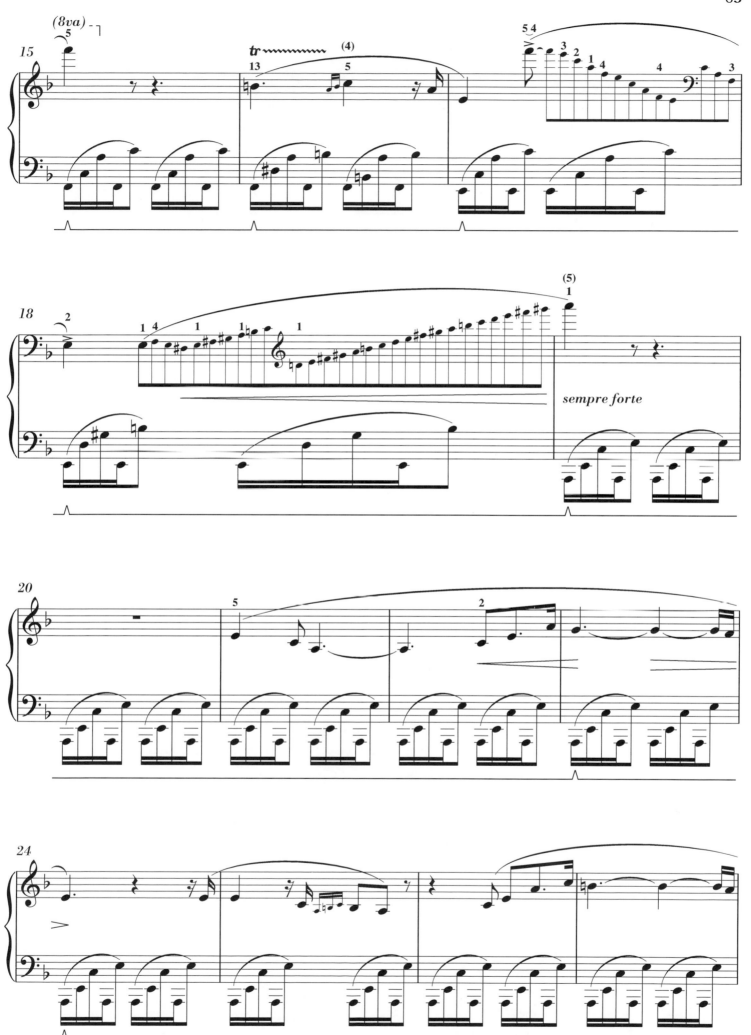

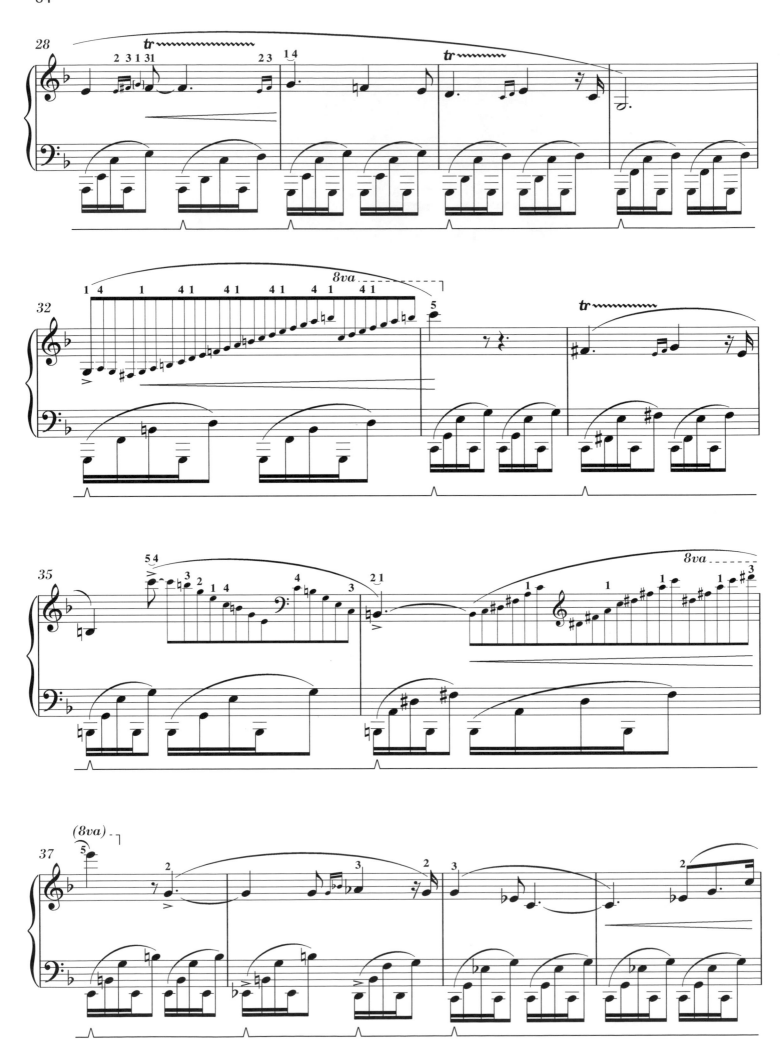

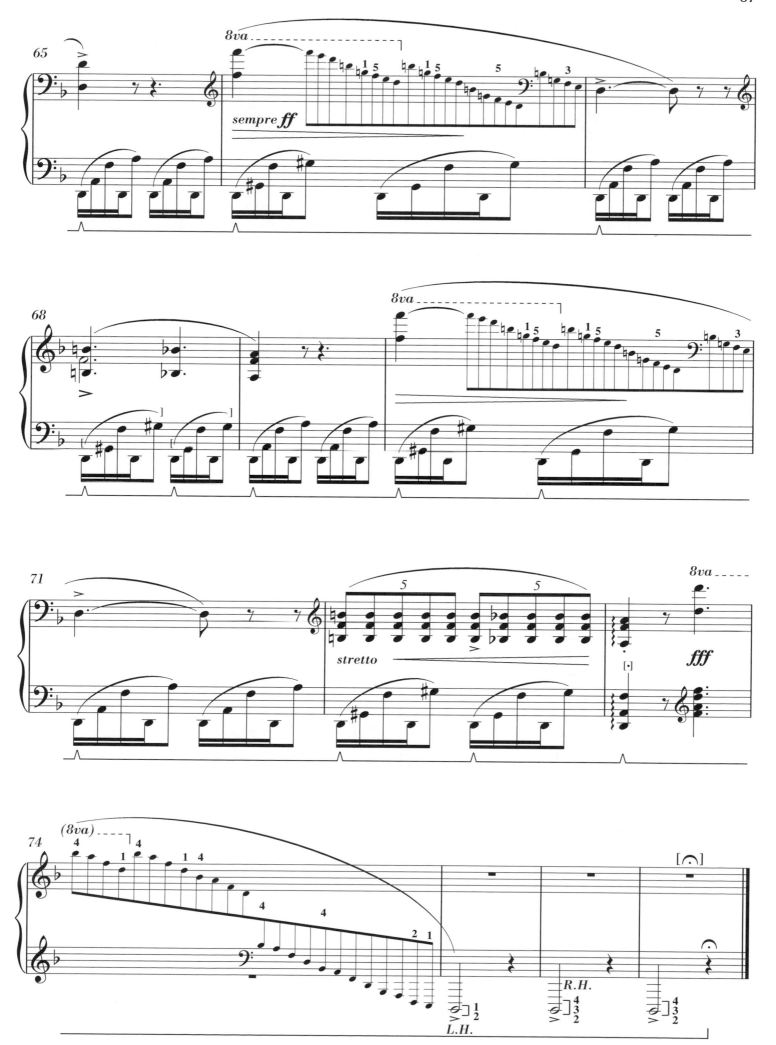

A Mademoiselle la Princesse Elisabeth Czernicheff

Prelude in C-sharp Minor

Frédéric Chopin
Op. 45

A mon ami Pierre Wolff

Prelude in A-flat Major

Frédéric Chopin

ABOUT THE EDITOR

BRIAN GANZ

Brian Ganz is widely regarded as one of the leading pianists of his generation. After he performed the *Preludes* in an all-Chopin recital in Washington D.C., the *Washington Post* declared, "One comes away from a recital by pianist Brian Ganz not only exhilarated by the power of the performance but also moved by his search for artistic truth."

Mr. Ganz was winner of one of two First Grand Prizes awarded in the 1989 Marguerite Long-Jacques Thibaud International Piano Competition in Paris. That same year, he won a Beethoven Fellowship awarded by the American Pianists Association, and in 1991 he was a silver medalist with third prize in the Queen Elisabeth of Belgium International Piano Competition. After his performance in the finals of the Brussels competition, the critic for *La Libre Belgique* wrote, "We don't have the words to speak of this fabulous musician who lives music with a generous urgency and brings his public into a state of intense joy."

He has appeared as soloist with such orchestras as the St. Louis Symphony, the St. Petersburg (Russia) Philharmonic, the City of London Sinfonia, L'Orchestre Lamoureux, and L'Orchestre Philharmonique de Monte Carlo, and has performed under the baton of such conductors as Leonard Slatkin, Mstislav Rostropovich, and Pinchas Zukerman. He made his recording debut in 1992 for the Gailly label in Belgium, and his recordings of works of Chopin and Dutilleux have been released on the *Accord* label in Paris. In 2001, he began a project with *Maestoso Records* in which he will record the complete works of Chopin.

Mr. Ganz is a graduate of the Peabody Conservatory of Music, where he studied with Leon Fleisher. Earlier teachers include Ylda Novik and the late Claire Deene. Gifted as a teacher himself, Mr. Ganz is Artist-in-Residence at St. Mary's College of Maryland, where he has been a member of the piano faculty since 1986. In 2000, he joined the piano faculty of the Peabody Conservatory. He lives in Annapolis with his wife Tatiana Johanning and their son, Dylan.